Design a Dish

Save Your Food Dollars!

Disclaimer

I am not a healthcare professional. I am a mom who believes that we are on the correct path for providing nutrient-dense nourishing foods. You should do your own research and come to your own conclusions for your healthcare and nutrition, along with consulting a healthcare professional. I highly recommend contacting the Chapter Leader of your local Weston A. Price Foundation to ask about a list of healthcare providers.

This text contains affiliate links for Traditional Cooking School by GNOWFGLINS (TraditionalCookingSchool.com). If you make a purchase that originated from this document, I will receive a small commission. Your cost will be the same, and I greatly appreciate your support!

Copyright 2012, 2013, 2018, 2020 Millie Copper

ISBN-13: 978-1-7327482-0-0

All Rights Reserved

Material is not to be copied, shared, or republished without prior written consent of the author. All methods/formulas are original or noted as inspired/adapted.

Table of Contents

Design a Recipe 1
Design Your Ingredients 11
Design a Muffin 14
Design a Sourdough Muffin 25
Design a Soup/Stew 33
Design a Casserole 44
Design a Crock Pot Dish... 51
Design a Meatloaf Burger, Ball, or Brat.............................. 58
Design an Egg Entrée 67
Design a Meat Salad... 87
Design a Salad Dressing... 96
Design a…? 102
Resources.. 107
Meet the Author 111

Dedicated to my mama.

Design a Recipe

With today's volatile economy, most people are pinching pennies, and the food budget tends to be one of the first items cut.

Providing nutritious and healthy meals doesn't have to blow your budget.

One of the best ways to stretch your food dollar is by learning how to design or create your own recipes or methods. Using a general method for cooking, which you can personalize with ingredients that are less expensive or abundant *to you*, will help you realize the biggest savings on your food bill.

This is a concept that I learned young but didn't realize I was learning it. My mama rarely used a recipe to create meals. I can't say we ever ate gourmet-style foods, but they were filling and, especially when I was quite young, made from real food ingredients.

I lived on a dairy farm as a young girl. We had an abundance of fresh milk and cheeses since those were part of the "perks" of a dairy farm. Since money was often tight on a hired dairyman's salary, other ingredients were rather frugal.

I remember lots of pinto beans, some ground beef (also part of the dairy farm perks), and assorted pastas, along with the very rare sweet treat in the form of homemade cakes or pies. Even with these limited ingredients, we still had a nice variety of meals.

The reason for this? My mama was very creative at changing simple ingredients into different meals.

Fast forward to my early days as a young (broke) wife. I had learned these basic cooking skills from my mama but thought they were not "good enough." I tried every new recipe in whatever cooking or women's magazine that came along. This often resulted in me buying special ingredients that were only used that one time—wasting money.

Somehow, I came across the book *The Complete Tightwad Gazette* by Amy Dacyczyn. In this book she shares the article "Create a Muffin Breakfast" and states "...blindly following recipes won't help you save the maximum amount on your food bill."

This was a huge *ah-ha* moment for me. I realized that maybe my mama was onto something. Don't get me wrong, I still use recipes and think they're wonderful, but most of the food cooked in my kitchen is created by following methods or formulas instead of a written-out recipe.

These formulas are a great way to really stretch your food dollars since they work with the ingredients that you need to use up or that you have in abundance.

In this eBook, I'll be sharing some of my favorite methods. I'm sure you already use some of these methods in your kitchen.

My hope is this will give you even more inspiration and guidelines for designing your own recipes and basic formulas.

I am confident that by utilizing this skill you will see a decrease in your overall food bill and enjoy a wide variety of meals and flavors.

Keep in mind, most of these meals will not be gourmet but will be wonderful, simple dishes that you can prepare day in and day out.

You'll be amazed how easy it is to nourish your family with these tasty dishes! I put together a price book, which helped me determine when I was getting something for a great price. I also used it to keep track of when things went on sale. All of this was very helpful with stocking the pantry.

I was very comfortable with using the pantry principle, and I planned our meals based on what we had on hand. Then I'd make a shopping list to pick up any other needed items, such as fresh produce or the occasional specialty ingredient.

Then, one day, I read an article about someone who took their pantry to a whole new level—way beyond anything I knew. That was when I was introduced to food storage.

I found the concept of food storage to be very interesting. I started researching food storage but didn't spend too much time on it. So much of the information that I found led me to believe food storage was the idea of buying a large amount of food (most places recommend a year supply) and storing it away until some major disaster happened and it was needed.

I have to admit, that didn't appeal to me at all. The recommended items to store weren't foods I was familiar with. I had no idea how to even cook most of the things! I put the idea of food storage out of my head and happily continued stocking my pantry. After all, while we couldn't "survive" on our pantry, we did have many weeks of food available to us. Yep, those many boxes of rice mix would get a little old, but I didn't worry about that.

In December of 2007, we had a wake-up call.

We lived in the Pacific Northwest when the Great Coastal Gale hit. On Sunday, the electricity went out. Monday morning, my husband left for work and returned about ten minutes later. Every road between our house and the highway was blocked by fallen trees. The wind was blowing something awful, but we didn't know it was blowing as bad as it was due to the location of our house.

We lived on the edge of a forest, and the number of downed trees was incredible. And with the wind still blowing and trees still falling, it was too dangerous to try to move the trees so Joe could go to work.

To top it off, the phones didn't work. Landlines and cell phones were both gone. We had a wind-up radio, but the local radio station wasn't transmitting. No power, no phone, no news, and no way out was an interesting place to be.

The following day, the wind had subsided, and after working with the chainsaw-carrying neighbors, we were able to get to the highway.

Town was seventeen miles west. None of the neighbors had been into town, and no one really knew what was going on. Both Joe and I wanted to check in with our employers since the phones were still out. My work was on the way to town, and Joe's was in town. The highway to town was covered in debris but passable.

Town was a disaster. Many, many shop windows had been blown out. There was no power. No gas stations were open. There was a grocery store open, accepting cash only and escorting people to a specially stocked area with a flashlight. Restaurants were closed. The banks were closed. (The next day, our bank reopened—sort of—and people could take out only $100 until the power came back on.) Plus, it was the beginning of the month and many people, including us, were expecting paychecks. Most paychecks are made in a computer, and without power, paychecks couldn't be easily figured and printed. And without the banks open, money couldn't be retrieved from those paychecks. It really was quite a mess.

The power started coming back on, the phones once again worked, and things started to reopen. At home, our power came back on Friday.

Things were starting to get back to normal when we had a setback. Due to the storm, a hillside gave way on one of the main roads into our town. That mudslide closed the road for several weeks. There was a noticeable drop in the restocking of depleted supplies while the road was closed.

Our event could've been worse as far as disasters go. There was loss of life, and our county was declared a disaster area, so it was bad enough. Major earthquakes, tsunami, tornadoes, and hurricanes happen often. I'm sure we're all familiar with Hurricane Katrina and other, more recent hurricanes.

Because of our food on hand, we weren't affected by the short-term power outage and lack of shopping. But we did notice that we didn't have a very good variety. I was wrong about enjoying those boxes of rice for any amount of time.

We were also fortunate to have water while the power was out. A town down the road from us was not so fortunate. The wind had knocked over a tree and taken out something important that made the water arrive at people's homes. They were out of water for several days before the repairs were made.

After the storm, I started searching out more information on food storage. While we weren't really affected by the few days of power outage, another few weeks of no power and we would've worried about our food supply. Plus, our choices would become quite limited. Storms of that magnitude weren't common in our area, but the fact that it did happen was a huge wake-up call.

I started learning about food storage and sharing what I learned with my husband. To be quite honest, Joe was not 100 percent on board, but he said if I thought it was a good idea then to go ahead. That was before our real food journey had started, so my pantry stocking consisted of the standard items recommended by "survival" websites: shortening, lots of canned goods, and other similar items. I did get a small amount of whole wheat after Joe gifted me with a crank grain grinder, but that was the closest to a whole food item we had in our pantry. We built our pantry fairly well, to a point where we'd be good for a couple of months. Then things changed for us, and we moved. We stopped buying food and started eating what we had. By the time we settled in Wyoming, our stocked-up food was gone, and we were beginning our real food journey.

It took us a while to rebuild our pantry. Our money was tight, but we tried to put a few dollars toward extra things each month.

My big hang up was, what should we put in our pantry now that we eat real food?

By definition, real food is fresh food. It spoils. It took me a good year to get a handle on exactly *what* we wanted to store in our real food pantry.

Like before, Joe was okay with the idea but not overly excited. He agreed that buying things in bulk at a low price made good financial sense. He agreed that having a well-stocked pantry with food on hand would cut down on trips to town. He agreed that our Wyoming weather could make driving to town difficult some days—we've had snow drifts in our yard that were so high I was unable to get the car out for days. But he cautioned me not to "go nuts." He didn't want me buying so much food that it'd go bad before we could use it. We decided to build up three months' worth of food, plus a little more during the winter. That seemed like a reasonable amount that we could easily store and use.

Our real, whole, traditional foods diet focuses on consuming the highest quality ingredients that our budget allows. This often means we purchase these items from as close to the source as possible. Our beef comes from local ranches, our eggs local farms—well, ours actually come from our own chickens. We buy grains from either local farmers or through a bulk buying situation. Our produce is from the seasonal farmers market, our own garden, gardens of others, our buying club, or the local health food store. We also order several items online. We buy some things from major supermarkets, but those numbers are small.

Stocking your pantry for the lowest amount of money possible does take some effort, but it can be done! Depending on your own personal goals, you may be able to build a wonderfully stocked real food pantry that will save you money and time, and give you peace of mind.

Design Your Ingredients

I believe it's important to note that starting with the best-quality ingredients you can afford is important.

What does best quality mean?

In our house, we choose grass-fed (and finished) beef, free-range poultry (ours are homegrown), eggs from free-range hens (also homegrown and truly free-range), wild game, organic produce for items that are high spray, and sometimes organic grains and legumes. We also pick traditional fats such as butter, duck or chicken fat, coconut oil, palm oil, and olive oil—and we eat these fats liberally!

What if your budget is too tight to afford grass-fed beef, free-range chicken, etc.? Or what if these items are not available in your area? Then you should choose the best option available to you that fits within your budget.

In addition to your base ingredients, having a variety of herbs, spices, and seasonings will go a long way toward adding excitement to your basic dishes.

Sea salt and pepper are great, but spicing things up a bit with dried or fresh herbs or spices with a bit of a kick can change an ordinary meal into something extraordinary. Using different spices, you could easily eat chicken every night and not feel like you're eating the same old boring thing night after night. A chicken dish flavored with chili and cumin tastes nothing like a chicken dish flavored with curry.

A few miscellaneous ingredients are always nice. While we do strive to eat a real, whole, traditional foods diet, we do keep some canned goods on hand to help with our meals. Coconut milk, tomatoes, tomato sauce and paste, canned fish, teriyaki or Pad Thai sauce, and ketchup (without high-fructose corn syrup), are just a sample of items we keep in our cupboard. You may or may not choose to keep these kind of things in your real food kitchen.

You may notice that many of my formulas suggest a "topper." These toppers take what starts as an ordinary meal and really kicks it up.

A humble bowl of soup is definitely more appealing with a dollop of sour cream on top.

Many of these toppers are a lacto-fermented or cultured product. This provides a great way to add healthy probiotics into a meal, which are so wonderful in aiding in digestion and gut health.

Toppers can also be a bit of a sneaky way to add these ferments. My children are much more likely to eat sauerkraut when it's part of a dish as opposed to sitting alone on the plate.

Keep in mind, when using fermented or cultured toppers, you don't want them to get hot. That will kill all the good stuff in them. If topping a hot dish, allow that dish to cool a little first.

When our budget allows, we also keep a few "goodie style" components to add to some of our formula meals.

This might be something like almonds, peanuts, pimentos, olives, artichoke hearts, fresh cilantro, etc.

These aren't necessary but are a very nice addition.

A simple skillet dish of leftover rice, soy or teriyaki sauce, chopped veggies, and scrambled eggs (essentially, fried rice) can become something special when almonds or peanuts and fresh cilantro are added to the top. Likewise, a casserole with a little pimento or artichoke hearts always makes a big impression on my family.

Design a Muffin

Just like my inspiration from Amy Dacyczyn in *The Complete Tightwad Gazette*, an adaptable muffin formula is an important component in my kitchen.

The formula in the Gazette uses standard ingredients. My muffin formula has been modified to incorporate soaking the grains—to aid in digestion and reduce phytic acid and other antinutrients—and uses healthy fats.

I originally shared my Design a Muffin idea on a family blog. I was quite honored when Wardee from GNOWFGLINS tweaked my version and shared it on her blog, plus included it in her Fundamentals eCourse. The version I share is my method. (Please check the Resources at the end of this book for a link to Wardee's website.)

Required Ingredients

Grain: Use 2 to 2 ½ cups whole wheat flour. Or substitute oatmeal, cornmeal, or rye flour for the whole wheat flour. My best results come from 1 cup whole wheat flour and 1 cup old-fashioned rolled oats.

Liquid: 1 cup, you want a liquid that will do two jobs. First, it will act as the liquid to bind all of your dry ingredients together, just like in any muffin. Second (and maybe more important?) you want a liquid that will be slightly acidic in order to help reduce the phytic acid and other antinutrients that are naturally occurring in your grain(s).

You can use yogurt, kefir, or buttermilk for your already acidic liquid. Or you can use milk and an addition such as whey, kombucha, apple cider vinegar, kefir, or lemon juice. Add 1 tablespoon of acidic medium for each cup of liquid.

You can also do what I often do and use water for half of your liquid. Example: use ½ cup yogurt and ½ cup water to total 1 cup; or ½ cup milk, ½ cup water, plus 1 tablespoon whey. You can use plain water plus your acidic medium for a less rich but still delicious muffin if that is what you have available.

Fat: Use ¼ cup melted butter or coconut oil. Or you can substitute an all-natural nut butter for all or part of the fat. Another thing that works well is using a "wet addition" for all or part of the fat. For a savory muffin, you might try olive oil as your fat.

Egg: Use one egg. This goes back to using the best-quality ingredients you can afford. Pastured or free-range eggs are great if possible.

Sweetener: Use up to ½ cup of a natural sweetener. You could use Sucanat, Rapadura, honey, maple syrup, blackstrap molasses, evaporated cane juice, or a combination of any of these.

Keep in mind that honey, maple syrup, and molasses are liquid. Use caution when using these in combination with wet additions so your batter does not become overly wet. I've had excellent result using as little as 2 tablespoons of sweetener, especially when combined with additions that are on the sweet side.

When using honey, I always use less than I would something like Sucanat. I keep honey around ¼ of a cup. If making a savory muffin, use only 2 tablespoons or eliminate completely.

Baking Powder/Baking Soda: Equal amounts of both work well for me. You could choose to only use baking powder, but I find that the soda works well with the slight acidity of the soaking liquid.

Sea Salt: Use ½ teaspoon of sea salt.

You could stop here and make your muffins *plain*. I've made plain muffins before, and they turned out great. But one of the really fun things about a method like this is the ability to customize the muffins by using items you have on hand.

Optional Additions

These can be used in any combination you wish.

> **Dry Additions:** Chopped crispy nuts (almonds, peanuts, pecans, or walnuts), sunflower seeds, raisins, shredded coconut, etc. Poppy seeds are also a nice dry addition. I usually use 2 tablespoons.
>
> **Moist Additions:** Blueberries, chopped or shredded apple, sautéed apples, freshly shredded zucchini, shredded carrots, etc.
>
> **Wet Additions:** Pumpkin puree, applesauce, mashed banana, cottage cheese, cooked and mashed sweet potato, cooked and mashed carrot, frozen zucchini

that has been thawed and drained, home canned fruit that has been drained and cut in chunks, or fruit juice (lemon, lime, orange—as a flavoring only).

Note: When using wet ingredients, your muffins can get quite wet. This can cause the need for additional baking time. To help eliminate this, I keep the wet ingredients to no more than ½ cup.

Spices: Use 1 to 4 teaspoons, depending on your preferences, of one spice or a combination of spices, such as cinnamon, nutmeg, ground ginger, cloves, grated orange peel, grated lemon peel, etc. One option for spices is to use cinnamon sugar (cinnamon mixed with Sucanat or other dry sweetener) and sprinkle it on the top of the muffins before baking. This is very good!

All-Natural Fruit Spreads: Here's an idea for a nice change of pace. Fill the muffin cups half full with plain batter, add a teaspoon of fruit spread, and then top with 2 more teaspoons of batter. My children love this.

Savory Muffins: These make a nice accompaniment to a simple soup dinner. Use only 2 tablespoons of sweetener or omit entirely. I've had excellent results using a combination of whole wheat flour and rye flour, or whole wheat flour and cornmeal (1 cup each).

For additions, use things like shredded cheese (½ cup), a few strips of fried and crumbled bacon (we use turkey or beef bacon), and 2 or 3 tablespoons of any or all of the following: minced or grated onion, shredded zucchini, finely chopped leftover cooked vegetables (I like broccoli), Parmesan cheese, or fresh herbs of your choice. If using dried herbs, use 1 to 2 teaspoons.

How to Design a Muffin

Soak It: Combine your choice of grain(s) and your liquid in a bowl. Don't forget your acidic medium if using milk or water. Allow to soak, covered, at room temperature for a minimum of seven hours.

Mix In: After your soaking time is up, mix in your egg and oil. The first time you make this, it's going to seem all wrong. The batter that has soaked all day will be thick and seem very hard to mix. I usually mix in one egg, and when that blends well, I slowly start adding any additional eggs (when making multiple batches) and the oil.

Don't be tempted to add additional soaking liquid when you start out. You want that batter to be thick so your muffins turn out with a beautiful amount of rise. I've tried a thinner batter, hoping for easier mixing, and ended up with muffin pancakes.

Add any moist or wet ingredients to the batter, such as honey, molasses, vanilla, etc. Hold off on adding things like blueberries until the two bowls are combined so they don't turn to mush. No one likes mush berries.

Separate Bowl: Combine the dry ingredients in a separate bowl. Go ahead and put any spices or dry additions into this bowl.

Combine: Combine the two bowls until mixed. Occasionally, the mixing will be challenging and you might have "bits" of grain that don't combine. I don't worry too much about this and just do the best I can. Your finished product might have spots of a slightly different color, but it will still taste great. Stir in any final additions such as blueberries.

Bake: Put your muffins into prepared muffin tins. Bake in a 400-degree oven for 18 to 25 minutes. Your baking time may vary depending on how wet your batter is and your altitude. I usually set the timer for 18 minutes, then check them every three to five minutes afterwards until a toothpick comes out clean.

I rarely make a single batch of muffins. I like to save energy and time by making a double—or larger—batch. These muffins keep very well when covered, or they can also be stashed in the freezer for future use.

Tasty Combinations

After several years of designing our muffins, we've developed some favorites.

> **Lemon Poppy Seed:** When we want muffins or breakfast cake and I have nothing on hand that needs to be used up, I make a lemon poppy seed. My only additions are 2 tablespoons of poppy seeds, 2 tablespoons of lemon juice, 1 teaspoon each of ground cinnamon and ground ginger, plus ½ teaspoon of nutmeg. Simple and delicious.
>
> **Peanut Butter Banana:** Bananas that are too ripe are very common here. (Seems I can never accurately estimate the banana consumption at my house; either I buy too few and they're gone too quick, or too many and they become too ripe.) My additions then become overripe bananas and peanut butter. I usually replace half of the fat with peanut butter.

(For ¼ cup fat, I'd use ⅛ cup peanut butter and ⅛ cup butter or coconut oil.) This makes a very tasty combination.

Now that you're familiar with the components to muffins, here is your formula. Let the experiments begin!

Basic Muffin Formula

(makes approximately one dozen)

> 2 to 2 ½ cups grain
> 1 cup buttermilk, yogurt, kefir, or milk with 1 tablespoon acidic medium

Combine your grain(s) with your liquid of choice. Cover with a cloth and let sit at room temperature for seven hours or overnight.

After your soaking time has completed, add and mix well:

> Up to ¼ cup fat
> 1 egg
> Up to ½ cup wet additions or 1 ½ cup moist additions (keep total additions under 1 ½ cup; do not add berries at this time)

In a separate bowl, combine:

Up to ½ cup sugar
1 teaspoon baking powder
1 teaspoon baking soda
½ teaspoon salt
Up to 1 ½ cup dry additions (keep total additions under 1 ½ cup)

Combine the two bowls until mixed. Add in berries or any other items you did not wish to become mush.

Bake in a 400-degree oven for 18 to 25 minutes. Your baking time may vary depending on how wet your batter is and your altitude.

Variation: Breakfast Cake

Instead of making muffins, put your batter in an 8-inch square pan or a loaf pan and sell it to your family as a "breakfast cake." I like doing this so I don't have to wash out each little muffin tin. A double batch fits perfectly in a 9 x 13 pan.

Watch your quantity when pouring into pans. Sometimes, your choice of ingredients will result in a batter that makes too much to fit in a pan without running over. Don't fill your pan more than ¾ full. When the batter exceeds the pan, put the remainder in muffin tins.

Do you only have enough batter to fill a couple of tins? No problem. Put water in the empty tins to avoid burning and to aid in cooking.

Muffins and breakfast cake are not just for breakfast. They also make a wonderful snack or light dessert!

Breakfast Cake with Yogurt "Frosting"

Design a Sourdough Muffin

Looking for a naturally leavened and completely delicious muffin?

Look no further!

These sourdough muffins are just as versatile as the soaked muffins. They have a wonderful sourdough flavor and are quite moist. My husband loves them since they turn out slightly denser than the soaked muffins.

If you want a slightly lighter muffin, add ½ teaspoon of baking soda to the combined batter before putting it in your muffin tins.

Note: Sourdough muffins and soaked muffins are very similar. Refer to the Design a Muffin section for Tasty

Combinations. One slight difference: I have never made a savory sourdough muffin. I believe it would work out just fine, but since I haven't made it myself, I'm not offering the suggestion in this section. Use the Design a Muffin section as a reference if you wish to try savory sourdough muffins.

Required Ingredients

Grain: Use 2 to 2 ½ cups whole wheat flour. Or substitute oatmeal, cornmeal, or rye flour for the whole wheat flour. My best results come from 1 cup whole wheat flour and 1 cup old-fashioned rolled oats.

Liquid: You'll need 1 cup of liquid. Water, milk, or half water and half milk appears to be the best choice for liquid in sourdough muffins. Unlike the previous muffin formula, you won't need to add an acidic medium. The sourdough starter will take care of that for you.

Sourdough Starter: Use ⅓ cup completely hydrated sourdough starter.

Fat: Use ¼ cup melted butter or coconut oil. Or you can substitute an all-natural nut butter for all or part of the fat. Another thing that works well is using a wet addition for all or part of the fat.

Egg: Use one egg.

Sweetener: Use up to ½ cup of a natural sweetener. You can use Sucanat, Rapadura, honey, maple syrup, blackstrap molasses, evaporated cane juice, or a combination of any of these.

Keep in mind that honey, maple syrup, and molasses are liquid. Use caution when using these in combination with wet additions so your batter doesn't become overly wet.

I've had excellent results using as little as 2 tablespoons of sweetener, especially when combined with additions that are on the sweet side. When using honey, I always use less than I would something like Sucanat. I keep honey around ¼ of a cup.

Sea Salt: ½ teaspoon of sea salt.

You can stop here and make your muffins *plain*. I've made plain muffins before, and they turned out great. But one of the really fun things about a method like this is the ability to customize the muffins with items you have on hand.

Optional Additions

These can be used in any combination you wish.

> **Dry Additions:** Chopped crispy nuts (almonds, peanuts, pecans, or walnuts), sunflower seeds,

raisins, shredded coconut, etc. Poppy seeds are a nice dry addition. I usually use 2 tablespoons.

Moist Additions: Blueberries, chopped or shredded apple, sautéed apples, freshly shredded zucchini, shredded carrots, etc.

Wet Additions: Pumpkin puree, applesauce, mashed banana, cottage cheese, cooked and mashed sweet potato, cooked and mashed carrot, frozen zucchini that has been thawed and drained, home canned fruit that has been drained and cut in chunks, or fruit juice (lemon, lime, orange—as a flavoring only).

Note: When using wet ingredients, your muffins can get quite wet. This can cause the need for additional baking time. To help eliminate this, I keep the wet ingredients to no more than ½ cup.

Spices: Use 1 to 4 teaspoons, depending on your preferences, of one spice or a combination of spices, such as cinnamon, nutmeg, ground ginger, cloves, grated orange peel, grated lemon peel, etc. One option for spices is to use cinnamon sugar (cinnamon mixed with Sucanat or other dry sweetener) and sprinkle it on top of the muffins before baking. This is very good!

All-Natural Fruit Spreads: Here's an idea for a nice change of pace. Fill the muffin cups half full of plain batter, add a teaspoon of fruit spread, and then top with 2 more teaspoons of batter. My children love this.

How to Design a Sourdough Muffin

Soak It: Combine your choice of grain(s), liquid, and starter in a bowl. Allow to soak, covered, at room temperature for a minimum of seven hours. I usually don't like to soak my sourdough muffin batter past 12 hours. It becomes a little "too sour" for my family past that point.

If I need to put off finishing my muffins (because it's been *one of those days*), I'll stash the batter in the fridge to slow down the souring process. This does make the mixing a little more challenging, but it keeps it from becoming too sour.

Mix In: After your soaking time is up, mix in your egg and oil. The first time you make this, it's going to seem all wrong. The batter that has soaked all day will be thick and seem very hard to mix. I usually mix in one egg, and when that blends well, I slowly start adding any additional eggs (when making multiple batches) and the oil.

Don't be tempted to add additional soaking liquid when you start out. You want that batter to be thick so your muffins turn out with a beautiful amount of rise. I've tried a thinner batter, hoping for easier mixing, and ended up with muffin pancakes.

Add any moist or wet ingredients to the batter, such as honey, molasses, vanilla, etc. Hold off on adding things like blueberries until the two bowls are combined so they don't turn to mush. No one likes mush berries.

Separate Bowl: Combine the dry ingredients in a separate bowl. Go ahead and put any spices or dry additions into this bowl.

Combine: Combine the two bowls until mixed. Occasionally, the mixing will be challenging and you might have "bits" of grain that don't combine. I don't worry too much about this and just do the best I can. Your finished product might have spots of a slightly different color, but it will still taste great. Stir in any final additions such as blueberries.

Bake: Put your muffins into prepared muffin tins. Bake in a 400-degree oven for 18 to 25 minutes. Your baking time may vary, depending on how wet your batter is and your altitude. I usually set the timer for 18 minutes and then check them every three to five minutes afterwards until a toothpick comes out clean.

I rarely make a single batch of muffins. I like to save energy and time by making a double, or larger, batch. These keep very well when covered, or they can also be stashed in the freezer for future use.

Basic Sourdough Muffin Formula

(makes approximately one dozen)

> 2 to 2 ½ cups grain
> 1 cup liquid
> ⅓ cup fully hydrated sourdough starter

Combine your grain(s) with liquid and starter. Cover with a cloth and let sit at room temperature for seven hours or overnight.

After your soaking time has completed, add and mix well:

> Up to ¼ cup fat
> 1 egg
> Up to ½ cup wet or 1 ½ cup moist additions (keep total additions under 1 ½ cup; do not add berries at this time)

In a separate bowl, combine:

Up to ½ cup sugar
½ teaspoon salt
Up to 1 ½ cup dry additions (keep total additions under 1 ½ cup)

Combine the two bowls until mixed. Stir in any berries or other items you do not wish to become mush.

Bake in a 400-degree oven for 18 to 25 minutes. Your baking time may vary depending on how wet your batter is and your altitude.

Variation: Breakfast Cake

Instead of making muffins, put the batter in an 8-inch square pan or a loaf pan and sell it to your family as a breakfast cake. Refer to the Design a Muffin section for further instructions.

Design a Soup/Stew

When the temperature drops, a hot bowl of soup really hits the spot. Believe me, with our Wyoming winters, we enjoy soup and stew quite often!

Soup is also a wonderful way to use up leftover ingredients. By starting with nutrient-rich bone broth, an incredibly nourishing meal can be made with almost any combination of ingredients.

I usually construct my soups as I'm standing at the stove, viewing my soup pot as the perfect opportunity to use up those little bits that are hanging around in the fridge or freezer. This is a great way to help cut down on food waste, which in turn helps with reducing your food bill.

I use the word soup and stew interchangeably; I understand there is a bit of a difference. Usually, in my house, a soup is something I've pureed or made on the thin side. Our stews tend to be heartier and chunkier.

Sometimes I'll really throw my family for a loop and call our soup *chowder* or maybe even *chili*. Truly, they are all pretty much the same, and all are a wonderful way to extend your food budget.

Ingredients

Broth: It is my goal to have bone or meat broth readily available. Not the stuff that comes in a can or a cube, but homemade from real bones or real meat. Homemade broth or stock acts as a protein sparer. This allows you to consume (costly) meat less often and still maintain excellent health.

Making broth in a crock pot requires very little effort. Be sure to check out the Resources at the end of the book for different broth preparation methods.

Vegetables: Root vegetables are my first choice for soups and stews. Carrots, onions, and potatoes—which we almost always have on hand—are my go-to vegetables. Celery is great, too, but isn't something we often purchase. Sometimes I'll add tomatoes or tomato sauce or paste.

Shredded cabbage is spectacular in stews and adds an extra bit of heartiness.

Vegetables that have been left over from a previous meal make a wonderful addition to our soup pot. If you keep frozen vegetables on hand, they work well in soups and stews; this is an especially good way to use up partial bags.

Protein: My husband's first choice for protein in soups (or anything) is meat. I tend to agree with that thinking. I'll use raw stew meat if I have it on hand, but the bulk of our stews and soups are made from left over, already cooked meats.

I'll cook a roast or a whole chicken and specify a portion of that meat to use later in the week for soup. Making one meal and turning it into additional meals is a great way to save on time and money. We call these stretchy meals.

Sometimes I'll plan a soup where the protein is beans or even eggs, such as in an Egg Drop Soup.

We keep canned fish on hand (salmon, mackerel, tuna, sardines, clams, and oysters) and shrimp in the freezer, which are wonderful to add to a quick soup. Fish soup is usually when I throw that *chowder* word around.

On occasion, we'll have a soup that is just bone broth and vegetables. We usually puree this combination with our handheld blender to make a Cream of Vegetable Soup (more about this later).

Spices and Seasonings: Start with the basics: sea salt and pepper. Then think about the end result you would like to achieve. Do you want a taco-style soup or chili? Use chili powder, cumin, and cayenne pepper. Does Italian sound good? Use basil, garlic, and oregano. The sky is the limit! Spend a little time on Google learning about different flavor combinations and which spices go together.

Acid: A little bit of an acidic base really brightens up a soup's flavor. Lime juice is my favorite (about ¼ cup), but more often than not, I use fresh lemon juice or apple cider vinegar since we usually have those on hand. On the very rare occasion that I have wine available, I'll add that to the soup. If you feel the need to be proper, use red with beef and white with chicken. I tend to throw proper out the window and just pour in whatever I have.

I've also had great success with using kombucha as a flavoring. Please keep in mind that when heating kombucha you destroy the probiotic components of it, but as a flavor enhancer only, it's spectacular. If using wine, add it before the end of cooking so some of the alcohol can burn off. All other acids should be added at the very end when the soup or stew is removed from heat.

Additions

Dumplings: Depending on the soup, I might add dumplings. My family really loves these little biscuits that are cooked by the steam and the broth. See Resources for an easy and quick dumpling recipe.

Toppers: An easy way to take a simple soup to a new level is by adding something extra beyond the basics. Toppers are added after the soup is in the bowl.

Some toppers we like are sprouts, chopped green onions, shredded cheese, sourdough croutons, a slice of French or sourdough bread (or broken into bits), avocado, salsa, cilantro, your Design a Salad Dressing creation, clabber cheese, sour cream, or kefir cream. My husband also likes to add lacto-fermented sauerkraut to his soups.

Bases: Need to add a little more bulk to your soup? Put it over leftover cooked rice or pasta. Homemade noodles make a particularly wonderful base. Another great base is to put a slice of sourdough bread or a chunk of cornbread in the bottom of your bowl and put the soup on top of that.

Pureed Soups

A few years back, I bought a handheld blender for $15. It was a wonderful addition to my kitchen. We often have pureed soups, which are very reminiscent of creamed soups once sour cream, yogurt, or fresh cream are added to them.

In the book *Nourishing Traditions* by Sally Fallon and Mary Enig is a recipe for Cream of Vegetable Soup. I've used this soup as a guide to create creamy soups. Just about any combination of bone broth and vegetables make a wonderful creamy soup.

As of late, we've been enjoying using butternut squashes in our soups. Broth, butternut squash, and fresh ginger pureed together is wonderful. A great topping for this is the thick cream off of coconut milk. Just a small amount stirred in totally changes the flavor.

How to Design a Soup/Stew

I start with chopping up ½ to a whole onion and cooking it with a little coconut oil in my soup pot. If I'm using celery, I cook it along with the onion. I keep it over low heat and cook it until just soft (about 7 to 10 minutes). If I'm using uncooked stew meat, it goes in now to brown.

While that is cooking, I peel and chop the potatoes and carrots (I usually use three or four of each). Then, whatever other noncooked vegetables I'm using plus any precooked meat gets cut into bite-size pieces.

After my onions have cooked until just soft, I add in my broth (anywhere from ½ gallon to a full gallon, or occasionally half broth and half water). Now the carrots and potatoes go in so they can start cooking, and I add salt. I don't pre-salt my broth, so I'm pretty generous with it. I let the potatoes and carrots cook about 10 minutes.

Do I have other raw vegetables that need to go in? If so, I add them now and allow another five minutes or so of cooking time.

At this point, the carrots and onions have cooked a good 15 minutes and are just getting soft. Now is the time to add in any already cooked vegetables, the precooked meat, and seasonings. If I'm doing dumplings, those go on next (they take 20 to 30 minutes to cook).

If I'm not using dumplings, I cook the soup until the potatoes and carrots are soft and everything is heated through. That's it. These soups are fairly quick and easy since a good portion of the work (cooking the meat) has already been done.

Tasty Combinations

Pureed: When discussing pureed soups, I mentioned the broth, butternut squash, and fresh ginger combination. This is a very tasty soup!

Hearty: For a hearty stew, I like to load it up with vegetables. Onions, potatoes, carrots, and shredded cabbage, along with leftover roast or stew meat are very good. Add a can of tomatoes and a can of tomato sauce for extra richness. If you have wine, add a ½ cup (red is great, white will do, or you can substitute ¼ cup apple cider vinegar). Spice it up with chili powder, garlic, rosemary, and allspice.

Salmon Chowder: This is a good one! Lightly sauté a little onion and celery (if you have it) in a healthy fat. Add a couple of potatoes and carrots, both diced small. Add about 2 cups broth, salt, pepper, and some dried dill. Bring to a boil, then cook at a simmer until the potatoes and carrots are soft. Add a can of salmon (I crush the bones up) and 1 ½ cups of frozen corn (or one can of corn if this is something you keep in your pantry). Taste for seasoning, adjust if needed, and let it warm through. At the table, add a large dollop of sour cream or kefir cream to each bowl to give it a creamy, chowder finish. Top with shredded cheese. So good!

Speedy: The quickest soup I make is basically an Egg Drop Soup. First, sauté your onions. When soft, add a teaspoon or two of Garam Marsala (a wonderful blend of spices) and then add your broth. Bring to a boil. While that is heating, lightly beat up three eggs. Turn your broth down to medium. Add a few "chugs" of soy sauce, salt, and pepper to your broth. Taste it and adjust as necessary. When it tastes perfect, stream your eggs into the broth while stirring rapidly.

A Few Additional Thoughts

Let your personal tastes and budget determine how much meat you want to use in your soup; I use anywhere from ½ cup to 2 cups. Remember, if you're using a real bone broth, it acts as a protein sparer and you can use less meat.

I taste my soup or stew as I go along so the seasonings can be adjusted. I have a bad habit of never getting my salt right in soup, so this is necessary for me.

You don't have to be rigid in the way you make your soups. Only have chicken broth in the fridge but have leftover roast beef? No problem. Mixing your broth and meat is totally allowed.

Also allowed is mixing different types of meat. Do you have a ½ cup of beef and a ½ cup of chicken? Throw them both in! It will still be delicious.

Here's another really great thrifty tip from *The Complete Tightwad Gazette*: keep a container in the freezer to add any bits of leftover vegetables served with meals. When you're ready to make soup, toss the frozen or thawed veggies into the soup pot. You can also keep a container to put leftover meats in to use in the same manner. This is a great way to keep down food waste when you aren't in a soup mood.

Basic Soup/Stew Formula

>2 to 4 quarts broth
>2 to 4 cups vegetables
>½ to 2 cups meat
>Seasoning, herbs, and spices as desired
>¼ to ½ cup acid depending on type
>Additions: toppers as desired, base as desired

Cook onion, if using, in a little healthy fat over low heat until just soft (about 7 to 10 minutes). Add broth, salt, and hard vegetables (carrots, potatoes, etc.).

Allow to cook for 10 minutes.

Add any additional raw vegetables and cook five more minutes.

Add any cooked vegetables, precooked meat, and seasonings.

Allow to cook until heated through. If using dumplings, add those now and cook until done.

Put in bowls on top of your base, if using, and finish with toppers.

A Hearty Antelope Stew Topped with Sour Cream

Design a Casserole

Do you have an odd collection of leftovers but don't feel like making your trusty Design a Soup/Stew?

Perhaps the perfect alternative is to Design a Casserole.

Just like with the soup/stew option, this is a great way to help cut down on food waste, which in turn helps with reducing your food bill. The more tricks and tips in your arsenal, the more options you have for lowering your food cost.

Once again, I credit the original idea of adapting a casserole to the ingredients you have on hand (or are readily available) to Amy Dacyczyn, author of *The Complete*

Tightwad Gazette. In my version, I try to keep my ingredients real, whole, and traditional food friendly.

Ingredients

Starch: This can be prepared pasta, cooked white or brown rice, cooked quinoa, cooked spelt, wheat, or other grain, or peeled and very thinly sliced raw potatoes (shredded potatoes also work). I think millet would work too, but I have yet to try it. You want anywhere from 1 to 3 cups of starch, depending on the quantities of your other ingredients.

One thing I've discovered is, if you're using rice pasta, keep it very al dente. It gets soggy very easily. I do more of a par boil to it than actually cooking it, and then add just a smidge more liquid to my casserole so it can finish cooking and get soft—not soggy. Feel free to mix your starches as needed to equal 1 to 3 cups.

Vegetables: Use any combination of raw or leftover veggies. If you use carrots, you'll want to precook them when using something precooked as your starch. I aim for 2+ cups of vegetables.

Meat: Browned hamburger, leftover chicken, beef, venison, antelope (if you live in Wyoming!), etc., totaling ½ to 2 cups.

Binder: Lots of times a casserole will call for a can of cream of whatever soup. We don't use this since the ingredients are questionable and the taste is blah. You'll need a thick liquid to replace the cream soup and bind everything together. This could be homemade cream of whatever soup, homemade gravy, white sauce, tomato sauce, or even sour cream.

I figure on 1 ½ to 2 cups, knowing that I may need to add additional liquid if the mixture seems a bit dry. Use broth, milk, or water (¼ cup at a time) for your additional liquid.

Seasonings and Spices: I just put in whatever sounds good with the meat I'm using, plus sea salt and pepper. I think about the kind of end result I'm looking for, then spice accordingly. Do I want a taco-style casserole? If so, I'll use chili powder and cumin. Italian flavored? I'll use basil and oregano. For a curry style, I'll use lots of curry powder.

"Goodies": These are wonderful little treat additions just to add a little bit of a special touch to your casserole. They are mixed in with the casserole. Goodies could be pimento, olives, almonds, artichoke hearts, etc.

Topping: Cheese, breadcrumbs, properly prepared chopped or sliced nuts; these are added near the end of baking time.

What's a properly prepared nut? Nuts contain phytic acid and other antinutrients. Soaking will inhibit these and make the nuts more digestible. After soaking, dehydrate them in a dehydrator or oven to return the nuts to their crispy state.

Toppers: This is different than toppings. Toppers are put on after the casserole has been cooked. We usually just let each person put on their own toppers when serving. Great toppers are sprouts, chopped green onions, shredded cheese, avocado, salsa, cilantro, krauts or relishes, clabber cheese, sour cream, yogurt, your Design a Salad Dressing creation, etc.

How to Design a Casserole

Mix your combination of ingredients together, except the topping. Remember, if it seems a bit dry, add water, milk, or broth until it's moist. You don't want it wet, but you don't want it too dry either. After it's mixed, pour into a buttered casserole dish. (I usually make my casserole in a 9 x 13 pan.) Bake at 350 degrees for anywhere from 30 minutes to an hour or until everything is soft and warm throughout.

I usually add my toppings when I figure there's about 10 minutes of cooking time left. That way, the cheese can melt but not totally disappear. If you started with cooked rice or pasta, it will be done faster than if you started with raw potatoes. It's something important to keep in mind as you plan your cooking time.

Tasty Combinations

Beef and Rice: Leftover cooked rice, cooked carrots, corn, browned hamburger, beef broth gravy, and sliced almonds.

Beef and Veggie: Sliced potatoes, carrots, green pepper, corn, browned hamburger, tomato sauce, and cheese (see photo at beginning of chapter).

Chicken and Rice: Leftover cooked rice, onions and celery sautéed together in olive oil, precooked or leftover green beans, chicken (cut into bite-size pieces), thin white sauce, Parmesan cheese.

Basic Casserole Formula

1 to 3 cups starch
2 cups vegetables
½ to 2 cups cooked meat
1 ½ to 2+ cups binder (see notes)
Seasonings, spices, herbs
¼ cup goodie

Topping such as cheese, breadcrumbs, etc.

Toppers to add after plating

Mix your combination of ingredients together, except the topping. Remember, if it seems a bit dry, add water, milk or broth until it's moist. You don't want it wet, but not too dry either.

After it is mixed, pour into a buttered casserole dish. (I usually make my casserole in a 9 x 13 pan.) Bake at 350 degrees for anywhere from 30 minutes to an hour or until everything is soft and warm throughout. Add topping when there is about 10 minutes of cooking time left.

Variation: Pot Pie

Here is a wonderful change to a standard casserole.

Omit the starch, but consider potatoes to be a vegetable in this application. Precook potatoes and carrots in a little water until just soft.

Mix with any other veggies you wish to add, then mix in your meat, binder, seasonings, and goodie. Top with your favorite pie crust or biscuits. (Sourdough biscuits are wonderful.)

Delicious and Easy Pot Pie

Design a Crock Pot Dish

I usually refer to this as "Dump Dinner," but my husband let me know that does not sound very appetizing.

I like to make this with stew meat. We tend to have lots of stew meat—whether venison, antelope, or sometimes beef—and this is a great way to end up with a wonderfully tender meat.

This dish breaks down to three parts to make a complete meal: your wonderful crock pot component, a base, and a topper.

The crock pot part will have a bit of gravy with it, which is where the base comes in. I find having something to soak up that gravy is always wonderful.

You already know of my affection for toppers and how we use them to add probiotics and a little kick to our meal—that's no different with crock pot dishes.

Liquid and spices are what make this meal very adaptable. You can vary your flavor by changing your liquid. I offer suggestions below.

Ingredients

Meat: I usually use stew meat, but you could certainly use chunks of chicken breast or roast instead.

Veggies: Almost any veggie will work in this—chop into bite-size pieces or shred cabbage. Keep in mind, this will be cooking all day. You don't want to use a veggie that will get too soggy during that time. I don't often use potatoes since they make a great base, but you can certainly use them.

Potatoes, carrots, beef, coconut milk, and curry powder would be quite delicious served over rice. Somewhat like a Massaman Curry.

Liquid: There are so many options here! Let your tastes and what you have available be your guide.

- Tomato sauce or tomato paste are super easy; just open the can or jar and pour it in. If using paste, add water to thin.
- Coconut milk is also easy. Open can and pour in or use your homemade coconut milk.
- Gravy is great but does require a little planning ahead. The night before, mix together ½ cup of whole wheat flour, ½ cup water, and 1 tablespoon whey. Allow to stand at room temperature overnight (this is to reduce phytic acid and other antinutrients). The next morning, add either 1 ½ cups water or milk to the flour mixture. Stir to combine. Dump over the top of your meat and veggies in the crock pot. I love the milk gravy, but it freaks my kids out a little bit because the milk can sometimes curdle slightly while cooking. It still tastes great, just has little white bits.
- One slightly unusual (but delicious) liquid I've used before is leftover pickle juice. This is extremely good, but keep in mind, if you're using a pickle juice from a lacto-fermented pickle, you'll be getting the good flavor but not the probiotic benefits since the heat will "kill" it.

- Red wine, white wine, or kombucha also make great liquids. As with the pickle juice, the kombucha will be used for flavor only and not for the probiotic properties. When using wines, I add equal amounts of water.
- Your liquid could even be water. Just add a few extra spices for flavor/interest.

Spices: Think about what you want your final dish to taste like.

When using tomato sauce or paste, I tend to go with either Mexican flavored—using chili powder, cumin, a dash of cayenne pepper, garlic powder, salt, and pepper—or Italian flavored—using basil, oregano, garlic, salt, and pepper.

Coconut milk is wonderful with cumin, salt, and pepper. Plus, right before serving, stir in ½ to 1 cup of Nutritional Yeast. (Thank you to Wardee from Traditional Cooking School by GNOWFGLINS for introducing me to this combo.)

Curry is also nice with the coconut milk.

For the gravies, I tend to stay simple. Salt, pepper, garlic powder, and paprika are quite nice.

Pickle juice is so good on its own that I only add salt and pepper.

How to Design a Crock Pot Dish

Dump: Put in your stew meat, dump your veggies over the top, and add the liquid. Finish with adding in your spices. Give it a quick stir and turn your crock pot on low. It'll be ready six to eight hours later. I've found this is a very forgiving dish. I've started it early in the morning and not gone back to it until 10 hours later with zero problems.

Base: Your crock pot dish has some sort of gravy and begs for something underneath to soak it all up.

This does not get added to the crock pot.

The base goes on your plate (or in a bowl) and the crock pot component goes over the top. Some bases we use are boiled baby red potatoes, mashed potatoes, fried potatoes, rice (white or brown), quinoa, millet, and pasta (homemade sourdough pasta is wonderful).

Toppers: My family likes our toppers.

Sour cream is always a favorite. Other toppers that are great, depending on your desired flavor, are chopped crispy almonds or peanuts, cilantro, sprouts, shredded cheese, clabber cheese, sauerkraut, salsa, your Design a Salad Dressing creation, etc. The topping ideas are almost endless.

I really like to use toppers as a great way to get a probiotic into the meal, so I always offer at least one fermented or cultured topping.

Tasty Combinations

To be honest, I have yet to find a combination that I don't like!

Italian Style: The picture above was beef, shredded cabbage, onion, tomatoes, tomato sauce, basil, oregano, garlic powder, sea salt, and pepper. This was served with a quinoa base and clabber cheese topper.

Kombucha Venison: I love the flavor of kombucha and venison. Add onions and fresh (or frozen) green beans, a little garlic, salt, and pepper. Serve over baby reds and top with sour cream. Yum!

Basic Crock Pot Dish Formula

Meat, can be frozen if using stew meat
1 to 2 cups assorted chopped veggies (carrots, onion, shredded cabbage, etc.)
Choice of liquid
Salt, pepper, and spices
Base

Toppings

Dump meat, veggies, liquid, and spices into the crock pot. Plug in and cook on low for seven to nine hours.

Put base in bowl or on plate, top with crock pot dish, and finish with toppings.

The Perfect Toppers! Sauerkraut and Cortido

Design a Meatloaf Burger, Ball, or Brat

These are home-cooked comfort foods! Many people make meatloaf and enjoy sandwiches the next day. This skips the meatloaf part and turns that yummy goodness into a burger, ball, or brat—your choice. It's a great way to stretch a pound of ground meat.

Whether you're making burgers, balls, or brats, the ingredients and the process remain the same. The change is in the shape of the final product.

Changing the shape and altering the ingredients slightly is also a wonderful way to avoid burnout. While I can eat hamburgers every night, my girls often commented "hamburgers again?" in a less than satisfied tone. Keep everyone happy with Italian meatloaf balls tonight, Gyro-style burgers tomorrow, and Chinese meatballs the next night. There are so many delicious varieties!

While ground meat tends to be economical, it still isn't cheap. Especially if you're choosing grass-fed meat. A one-pound package is at least $6 a pound. If you're making standard beef patties (burgers) out of this one-pound package, you can get four thin ¼-pound burgers or three decent ⅓-pound burgers. For most families, you'll need at least two pounds of ground meat to have a meal of burgers.

You can stretch this meat by making meatloaf burgers, balls, or brats! Adding some sort of grain and/or veggies is the key to making a moist and delicious burger, ball, or brat that stretches to feed everyone. Our entire family of five can enjoy filling meatloaf burgers from one pound of meat.

Ingredients

Meat: Any ground or minced meat: beef, pork, lamb, wild game (our most common meat), chicken, turkey, or a combination of the above.

You can even use a combination of meats.

Don't have any ground meat? Many times I mince stew cuts of wild game in the food processor to make my own "quick" grind. I use the pulse feature to get to the stage that I want. This works well for meatloaf burgers; I can add the rest of the ingredients and use the pulse feature to mix. Just don't over pulse. You want to keep a little texture to the mixture.

Tip: Add a small amount of ground liver to your meat to stretch it even farther and increase nutrition. Start with a small amount of liver (⅛ pound of liver per one pound of ground meat) and finely mince or process in a food processor. You can increase the amount of liver in future recipes if you desire.

Grain: This is the magic of the recipe! Adding a grain stretches the meat and makes the end product oh-so-tender.

Some grains you can use are:

- Leftover oatmeal, rice, cornmeal mush, or any cooked grain
- Soaked, uncooked grains (put to soak early in the day: 1 cup grain, 1 tablespoon acidic medium [see muffin recipe for more information], and 1 cup water)
- ½ cup flour (sprouted is best for reduced phytic acid)
- 1 cup fully hydrated sourdough starter

- Your favorite bread or cornbread cut in chunks, then moistened with a little milk to equal 1 cup

Produce: Finely minced onion is a must!

Also delicious (and a great way to stretch the meat) is grated carrot, grated potato, finely minced celery and/or finely shredded cabbage.

Fruit can also be an interesting addition. You can use dried fruits or fresh fruits finely minced. If the fresh fruit is wet, drain it for about half an hour in a colander and consider tossing it in flour. This helps keep the moisture manageable and the fruit separated. Raisins also benefit from a toss in flour.

Keep your produce addition to around 1 cup total. Feel free to mix and match!

Egg: At least one egg, but two may be needed. Start with one and see how it's all holding together. I've found that when using leftover cooked grains, sourdough starter, or bread/milk, one eggs is usually adequate. Uncooked grain or flour tend to need two eggs. If you're low on eggs, use one egg and 3 tablespoons milk or water.

Seasoning: This is the fun part! You have so many options here. Basil, fennel, peppermint, chili powder, cumin, oregano, parsley, and even a little hard cheese (like Parmesan) make a great flavor addition.

What flavor do you feel like tonight?

- Italian? Parsley, basil, and oregano are nice.
- Greek? Try fennel, marjoram, and oregano (go easy on each of these; about ¼ teaspoon).
- Asian? Powdered ginger, chives, and a pinch of red pepper flakes.
- If you just can't decide what you're in the mood for, keep it simple with minced garlic or garlic powder, along with salt and pepper, for a nice lightly flavored burger, ball, or brat. This is also my choice when adding a sauce or gravy to my burger, balls, or brats.

How to Design a Meatloaf Burger, Ball, or Brat

Mix it: Add all your ingredients to a bowl and mix with the paddle attachment on your stand mixer, or (my favorite) mix with a wooden spoon or even your clean hands.

Shape it: Once everything is well blended, shape as desired.

>**Burgers:** Portion out into the needed number of patties. One pound of ground meat, with the grain and produce addition, will yield five to seven burgers.

Press into patties, forming them by hand. Or if you'd like uniform patties, use a lid (leftover from a jar of peanut butter or something a little larger than an average bun) covered with plastic wrap. Press the meat down inside the lid to fill. Voila! Uniform patties.

Balls: These are so fun! Roll out about 1 tablespoon of meat mixture for approximately 1-inch balls. You can scale this up or down depending on your end desires. Smaller balls are great in soup. Larger balls make an interesting main dish as an alternative to burgers. Yield varies depending on size.

Brats: Portion out into the needed number of brats. One pound of ground meat, with the grain and produce addition, will yield six to eight brats. Roll the portioned meat into a sausage shape. I like to keep them on the thinner side for easy cooking.

Chill: After you've finished shaping, move the meat to the refrigerator for 10 minutes. This helps them firm up and hold together better during the cooking process.

Note: Depending on your additions, they could still be quite fragile, so be gentle with them.

Cook: You have options again: oven-baked, pan-fried, or even grilled.

> **Oven-baked:** Heat oven to 425 degrees. Put burgers, balls, or brats on a parchment-lined cookie sheet (for easy cleanup) and bake at 425 for five minutes. Turn heat down to 375 degrees and continue baking to desired doneness; about 15 to 20 additional minutes.
>
> **Pan-fried:** Heat up your favorite cast-iron skillet. Add a little healthy fat (tallow, lard, or coconut oil works well here).
>
> - For burgers: cook on one side about six minutes until brown. Flip with a spatula and cook an additional three to five minutes to desired doneness.
> - For balls or brats: put in heated pan, leaving space between so they don't touch. Cook six to eight minutes, turning as needed to brown on all sides. You may have to cook in batches, especially when making balls.
>
> **Grill:** Preheat your grill.
>
> - For burgers or brats: Grill on one side to fully sear (about four minutes for a hot

grill), flip, and cook to desired doneness for an additional three to five minutes.

- For balls: These work best when threaded on a skewer and put in grill grates. Leave a little space between each ball so you don't end up with one long meatball. Cook four minutes on one side, then flip and cook an additional three to five minutes.

Tasty Combinations

Gyro Burger: Okay, so not a real gyro, but *sooo* good. This is especially tasty when using minced lamb or wild game. Use flour for your grain, two eggs, very finely minced onion and fresh garlic, minced parsley (fresh is great or rehydrated dried), 1 tablespoon oregano, salt, and pepper. Serve with a homemade Tzatziki sauce (or a simple dressing made out of yogurt and cucumbers) and wrapped in sourdough flatbread.

Jalapeno and Mango Brat: This one is inspired by a commercially prepared brat that we love. Unfortunately, the commercial version has MSG, and I feel terrible after eating it. Use very finely minced jalapeno (to keep the heat down, I only use ½ of a pepper and remove the seeds) combined with finely minced mango (drain for 30 minutes in a colander and toss with flour) along with minced onion, garlic, salt, and pepper. Delicious!

Basic Meatloaf Burger, Ball, or Brat Method

    1-pound ground meat
    1 cup wet grain or ½ cup flour
    Up to 1 cup produce
    1 or 2 eggs
    Seasoning

Mix all ingredients well to combine. Shape into desired shape. Chill for 10 minutes.

Bake, pan-fry, or grill and then enjoy!

Design an Egg Entrée

When spring arrives, my chickens take their egg-laying duties quite seriously!

As a result, we tend to have an overabundance of eggs. You may not have chickens laying their little hearts out, but eggs are a wonderful and inexpensive protein source.

In my area, eggs from free-range chickens sell for $3.00 to $3.50 a dozen. At less than 30 cents for one egg, that's a very reasonable price.

Knowing a few methods for creating a main dish egg entrée can really broaden your options while keeping your budget in check.

When thinking of an egg entrée, quiche is usually the first thing that comes to mind.

Once again, I learned my quiche making from *The Complete Tightwad Gazette* and her recipe for Universal Quiche. Of course, I do use some slightly different ingredients than she suggests, keeping with the real food theme. But overall, the concept is the same.

My biggest change is that I almost always make a crustless quiche. But you can certainly use your favorite pie crust recipe to make a crusted quiche.

Quiche

Crust: Omit or use your favorite pastry crust.

Eggs: Three to seven, depending on how large you want your quiche to be. Use three or four eggs for a pie plate, 8 x 8 pan, or cast-iron skillet; and six or seven eggs for a 9 x 13 pan (the size I make for my family).

Milk: This is to blend with the eggs and make your quiche richer and creamier.

You can use milk, coconut milk, cream, or even substitute half water for this. I use 1 cup milk (or ½ cup milk, ½ cup water) per three or four eggs.

Other options include using half of a thicker item such as sour cream, yogurt, kefir, mayonnaise, or cottage/clabber cheese and diluting with water—again, use ½ cup water plus ½ cup thicker item per three eggs.

As before, keep in mind that if using a cultured or raw product, you'll lose the probiotic benefits when cooking.

You can also use water in place of milk and still expect good results.

Cheese: Most quiche recipes call for cheese.

I'll admit, I *usually* add cheese in, but sometimes I don't.

I've found that if using a "creamy" vegetable, the cheese is not necessary. We'll talk more about this later.

If adding cheese, you want to use a hard, grated cheese such as cheddar, Swiss, or Monterey Jack; 1 to 2 cups are usually enough.

You can also use Parmesan cheese (very good), but you'll only need less than ½ cup of this style of cheese.

Filling: The sky is the limit on fillings!

You can use almost any combination of vegetables and/or meats. This is a great way to use up very small amounts of meats. A little goes a long way when minced into small pieces.

Leftover cooked fish also makes a nice addition, as does canned fish.

Don't have any leftover meat or fish? No problem. Eggs are a protein, so meat is not necessary. Use can vegetables only.

Leftover already steamed/cooked vegetables work great, as long as they aren't too liquid. What does this mean? You can use leftover spinach, but make sure to squeeze out any water.

I love to use onions in my quiche. To really bring out the onion flavor, caramelize the onion first by cooking it low and slow in butter or coconut oil.

Remember how I mentioned you could eliminate the cheese by using certain vegetables?

This is a wonderful tip shared by Jenny at Nourished Kitchen when she did her *Food Stamp Challenge* in October of 2009 (see Resources). She shared a recipe for Acorn Squash Custard. This is essentially a crustless quiche minus the eggs, and it tastes wonderful!

By using a creamy-style vegetable, such as mashed acorn squash, mashed sweet potato, or mashed butternut squash, you get a wonderful dish that's still rich and delicious without the cheese. Jenny even omits the milk addition in her version, but I still like the milk option since it allows me to use less eggs.

It is important to remember that whatever vegetables or meats you choose to use, these should be precooked prior to constructing your quiche.

I haven't had good results using uncooked fillings.

These can be steamed, sautéed, or roasted veggies or meats. Use any combination totaling 1 to 2 (or more) cups of filling.

Seasoning: Sea salt and pepper at the very least. Use any other herbs, spices, or seasonings that sound appealing and will go with your additions. I like dill when using fish; basil is great with roasted tomatoes and olives.

Toppers: As with so many other items, I like to put toppers on my quiche. Sour cream, clabber cheese, raw shredded cheese, and guacamole all make great toppers.

Construction: In a bowl, beat eggs with milk and add seasoning. If using a mashed item like squash or sweet potato, mix it in with the eggs.

Shred the cheese, if using. Cut, chop, or sauté the filling ingredients as needed.

When all your prep work is done, generously butter your cooking dish. (The cast-iron skillet used to caramelize the onions works wonderfully for a smallish quiche.)

Spread the filling evenly in the dish, then top with cheese. Pour egg mixture over the top and use a knife to wiggle the eggs in, to allow it to distribute evenly and spread throughout the filling and cheese.

Bake: Bake at 350 degrees for 35 to 45 minutes. You want the eggs to be just set. Remove from oven, setting aside for 5 to 10 minutes before cutting. This will give the eggs a chance to finish cooking and will also prevent it from drying out.

Tasty Combinations

> **Salmon/Dill:** This is very good. Use sautéed onions, leftover flaked salmon (or canned), salt, pepper, and dill.

Acorn Squash: The combination suggested by Jenny at Nourished Kitchen is certainly a family favorite. Caramelized onion and creamy acorn squash make a delightful combination.

Basic Quiche Method

>   3 to 7 Eggs
>   1 cup milk per 3 or 4 eggs
>   Up to 2 cups shredded cheese
>   Up to 2 cups filling
>   Seasoning

In a bowl, beat eggs with milk and add seasoning. If using a mashed item like squash or sweet potato, mix it in with the eggs.

Shred the cheese, if using. Cut, chop, or sauté the filling ingredients as needed.

Prepare your favorite pie crust, if using.

When all your prep work is done, place crust in your pie plate or baking dish, if making a crusted quiche. If you're making it crustless, generously butter your cooking dish.

Spread the filling evenly in the dish or on top of the crust, then top evenly with cheese.

Pour egg mixture over the top and use a knife to wiggle the eggs in to allow it to distribute evenly and spread throughout the filling and cheese.

Bake at 350 degrees for 25 to 45 minutes (cooking time may vary depending on your ingredients). You want the eggs to be just set.

Remove from oven, setting aside for 5 to 10 minutes before cutting. This will give the eggs a chance to finish cooking and will also prevent it from drying out.

Clafouti:

How about a sweet quiche?

These are commonly called a *clafouti*.

One slightly different thing with the clafouti compared to the crustless quiche is the addition of flour. Whole grain flour soaked the night before in an acidic liquid gives the dish an extra bit of firmness and body.

I've also had excellent results adding 1 tablespoon of coconut flour to my clafoutis (I've seen other recipes on the internet that suggest up to 3 tablespoons of coconut flour), but I've also left out flour altogether and it turns out fine.

Omitting the flour will result in a more custard-like dish, which will still be delicious!

Eggs: Three to seven, depending on how large you want your clafouti to be. Use three or four eggs for a pie plate, 8 x 8 pan, or cast-iron skillet; and six or seven eggs for a 9 x 13 pan (the size I make for my family).

Milk: This is to blend with the eggs and make your clafouti richer and creamier. You can use milk, coconut milk, cream, or even substitute half water for this.

I use 1 cup milk (or ½ cup milk and ½ cup water) per three or four eggs.

Other options include using half of a thicker item such as sour cream, yogurt, kefir, mayonnaise, or cottage/clabber cheese and diluting with water—again, use ½ cup water plus ½ cup thicker item per three eggs.

As before, keep in mind that if using a cultured or raw product, you'll lose the probiotic benefits when cooking.

Filling: Fruit of your choice—can be apples, pears, bananas, blueberries, etc. You can even mix your fruits, which I've had great results with.

I use about 1 cup of filling per three eggs. But to be quite honest, I estimate on this so that I'm not left with leftover apples, pears, or bits of banana (because then I would *have* to make muffins to use those up and we can't have that ☺).

Note: I have not had good results using frozen fruit. Once it heats up, everything becomes too liquid. After an hour of baking, it still tends to be a liquid mess.

If you wish to use frozen fruit, try thawing it first and straining out the extra liquid. Even so, you should still count on extra baking time.

Seasoning: Use sea salt plus a bit of natural sweetener. I use 2 tablespoons of sweetener per three or four eggs. Unless I'm using honey, then I only use 1 tablespoon because honey is sweeter.

Other things you can include are cinnamon, nutmeg, allspice, or other sweet spices. (Thank you, Erin D., for this suggestion.)

If you're using the flour addition, add this now. Be sure to read the notes below on flours that need soaking, or add 1 to 3 tablespoons of coconut flour for an instant and grain-free option.

Construction: Cut your fruit. Mix up your eggs and milk. Add your seasonings and sweetener to your egg/milk mixture. Evenly layer your fruit into the bottom of a buttered baking dish. Pour your egg mixture over the top. Use a knife to wiggle the eggs in to allow it to distribute evenly and spread throughout the fruit.

Tasty Combinations

We love clafouti as a breakfast and brunch item, or even as a dessert.

> **Apple Pear:** One apple and one pear sweetened with Sucanat. Yummy.
>
> **Banana Spice:** Banana plus nutmeg and cinnamon. I wasn't sure about adding the spices but decided to give it a try. Quite tasty!

Basic Clafouti Method

> 3 to 7 eggs
> 1 cup milk per 3 or 4 eggs
> Up to 2 cups fruit
> Flour (optional)
> Seasoning

In a bowl, beat eggs with milk and add seasoning. Add optional flour*. Cut fruit into bite-size pieces.

When all your prep work is done, generously butter your cooking dish. Spread the fruit evenly in the dish. Pour egg mixture over the top and use a knife to wiggle the eggs in to allow it to distribute evenly and spread throughout the fruit.

Bake at 350 degrees for 20 to 25 minutes (cooking time may vary depending on your ingredients). You want the eggs to be just set.

Remove from oven, setting aside for 5 to 10 minutes before cutting. This will give the eggs a chance to finish cooking and will also prevent it from drying out.

Optional flour options:

¼ cup whole grain flour (wheat, spelt, einkorn, etc.) whisked with ¾ cup water plus 2 tablespoons acidic medium (yogurt, kefir, kombucha, whey, clabber milk, vinegar, etc.) that has been covered and soaked at room temperature overnight.

OR

1 to 3 tablespoons coconut flour. This does not need to be soaked, so it's a great option for a quick meal.

Frittata

A discussion on main dish egg entrees would not be complete without mentioning frittatas.

This was something my mama used to make. She could be very creative with her frittatas too! I remember one that was green apple and bean sprout. An odd-sounding combination, but it was very good!

A frittata is cooked on the stove top and then finished in the oven. I find these to be the perfect fast food. I can have a frittata whipped up in less time than it would take to go through a drive-thru. And we won't even talk about the health differences.

I make my frittata in a cast-iron skillet. Sometimes, I make two of them (same or different flavorings).

Your frittata ingredients will look very much like your quiche ingredients. The main difference between a frittata and a crustless quiche is the cooking method.

I have yet to try using mashed squashes or sweet potato to make quiche, but I suspect it would work just fine. If you try it, be sure to let me know.

Grains such as leftover rice, quinoa, and cooked pasta all make very nice additions to a frittata and really add to the heartiness of the dish.

I have to admit that in our pre-real food days, I made many frittatas using ramen noodles (without the "flavor" pack). I wouldn't choose to use those now, but they did make a very substantial meal. Using real food ingredients, you'll have a much higher-quality substantial food.

Eggs: Three or four per skillet.

Milk: This is to blend with the eggs and make your frittata richer and creamier. You can use milk, coconut milk, cream, or even substitute half water for this. I use 1 cup milk (or ½ cup milk and ½ cup water) per three or four eggs.

Other options include using half of a thicker item such as sour cream, yogurt, kefir, mayonnaise, or cottage/clabber cheese and diluting with water—again, use ½ cup water plus ½ cup thicker item per three eggs.

As before, keep in mind that if using a cultured or raw product, you'll lose the probiotic benefits when cooking.

Cheese: Use a hard cheese such as cheddar, Swiss, or Monterey Jack; 1 to 2 cups are usually enough. You can also use Parmesan cheese (very good), but you'll only need less than ½ cup of this style of cheese. Grate the cheese for use.

Filling: The sky is the limit on fillings! You can use almost any combination of vegetables, grains and/or meats. This is a great way to use up very small amounts of meats. A little goes a long way when minced into small pieces.

Leftover cooked fish also makes a nice addition, as does canned fish.

Don't have any leftover meat or fish? No problem. Eggs are a protein, so meat isn't necessary. You can use only vegetables and/or grains.

Leftover already steamed or cooked vegetables work great as long as they are not too liquid.

What's this mean? You can use leftover spinach, but make sure to squeeze out any water.

As I mentioned with my mama's frittata, you can even use apples if you want.

Or instead of a savory frittata, how about a sweet frittata using fruits and adding sweetener (with or without cheese depending on fruits chosen)?

Grains should be already cooked. Long grains, such as spaghetti, can be cut into smaller pieces for better presentation and easier eating.

Seasoning: Sea salt and pepper at the very least.

Use any other herbs, spices, or seasonings that sound appealing and will go with your additions. I like dill when using fish; basil is great with roasted tomatoes and olives.

If making a sweet frittata, use a smidge of sea salt and a natural sweetener, plus cinnamon and/or nutmeg.

Toppers: As with so many other items, I like to put toppers on my frittata. Sour cream, clabber cheese, raw shredded cheese, and guacamole all make great toppers.

Construction: In a bowl, beat egg with milk, then add seasoning and cheese. Cut and chop your filling.

In a cast-iron skillet (or other skillet that can go in the oven), start sautéing your veggies (or fruit). I start with the onions and then build from there, thinking about the cooking time needed.

Once the vegetables are soft, spread the filling evenly in the dish.

Turn your heat to medium-low, and also turn your oven on to broil.

Pour egg mixture over the top and use a knife to wiggle the eggs in to allow it to distribute evenly and spread throughout the filling and cheese.

Then set your kitchen timer for five minutes. Leave the frittata completely alone for those five minutes.

Okay, so here's the thing with getting a frittata to cook evenly. You can't just leave it there to cook *after* those first five minutes. What you need to do is go around the edges and lift them up ever so slightly to allow the loose eggs to run down under the edge.

I do this every few minutes until it no longer runs freely.

Sometimes, if there's still quite a bit of loose egg, I'll pick the skillet up and move it so more egg runs under the edge (be sure to use a hot pad!).

When you think you have it to the point that it will no longer run, it's time to put the frittata under the broiler.

I never walk away from the oven after this point! That frittata that you have spent so much time on can go from not set to a black burnt mess in no time. Check it every couple of minutes.

The top will lightly brown, and it will all begin to puff up. Take it out of the oven and allow to set for five minutes or so to finish up.

Your frittata should be perfect!

Tasty Combinations

Onion, Rice, and Broccoli: Sautee onions, then add leftover rice and leftover/precooked broccoli that has been cut into bite-sized pieces. With the rice addition, this is a hearty dish.

Apple Pie and Cheddar: A delicious combination. Lightly sauté sliced apples, and when done, liberally sprinkle "pie" type spices on. Cinnamon, ginger, nutmeg, and allspice are great. Add shredded cheddar to the egg mixture (sharp cheddar is wonderful).

Basic Frittata Method

3 or 4 eggs

1 cup milk

Up to 2 cups shredded cheese

Up to 2 cups filling

Seasoning

In a bowl, beat eggs with milk, then add seasoning and shredded cheese. Cut or chop the filling ingredients as needed.

In a cast-iron skillet (or other skillet that can go in the oven), start sautéing your veggies (or fruit). Once the vegetables are soft, spread the filling evenly in the dish.

Turn your heat to medium-low, and also turn your oven onto broil.

Pour egg mixture over the top and use a knife to wiggle the eggs in to allow it to distribute evenly and spread throughout the filling and cheese.

Let cook without disturbing for five minutes.

Then, go around the edges and lift them up ever so slightly to allow the loose eggs to run down under the edge. Do this every few minutes until the egg mixture no longer runs freely.

When you think you have it to the point that it will no longer run, it's time to put the frittata under the broiler.

Check it every couple of minutes. When done, the top will lightly brown, and it will all begin to puff up.

Take it out of the oven and allow to set for five minutes or so to finish up. Your frittata should be perfect!

Design a Meat Salad

Are you looking for an extremely quick meal? Do you have just a little bit of leftover meat that needs to be used up?

Meat salad is the answer you are looking for.

Meat salad is another terrific way to add lacto-fermented and/or cultured foods into the meal.

Use lacto-fermented mayonnaise, homemade dressings (with cultured or lacto-fermented ingredients), cultured dairy products, lacto-fermented mustard, etc. Use a lacto-fermented pickle or relish as the crunch and/or the treat.

The options are really endless for you to add several probiotic ingredients to this dish.

Ingredients

Meat

    Beef, cooked and cubed
    Wild Game, cooked and cubed
    Chicken, cooked and cubed
    Turkey, cooked and cubed
    Salmon, cooked and flaked
    Canned tuna, salmon, mackerel, or sardines

I've had excellent results "mixing" my meats. Beef/game and chicken work just fine together. Salmon and tuna also go together just fine.

Crunch

    Celery, chopped
    Apple, cut into small pieces
    Cucumber, chopped
    Carrots, thinly sliced or shredded
    Mung bean sprouts
    Broccoli, cut into very small pieces
    Lacto-fermented pickles (from any vegetable), cut into small pieces

Any other veggie (or fruit) that sounds good to you, cut into bite-size pieces

Sauce(s)

Mayonnaise (homemade and lacto-fermented is best)
Sour cream
Yogurt
Clabber cheese
Kefir cheese
Basic soft cheese
House dressing (or your favorite flavor; homemade is best)
Mustard
Ketchup
Barbeque sauce or steak sauce
Combination of any of the above

Seasoning

Salt and pepper
Minced garlic or garlic powder
Curry
Chives
Herbs such as basil, oregano, dill, etc.

Sweetener such as Sucanat, honey, dehydrated cane sugar, etc.
Vinegar (apple cider or other favorite)
Combination of any of the above

Pretty much whatever sounds good to you.

Treat

Chopped or sliced crispy nuts
Sliced olives
Green onion
Diced avocado
Sauerkraut, kimchee, cortido, or ginger carrots
Pickle relish or other lacto-fermented relish
Cheese, shredded or cut into small chunks
Sweet pepper, cut into small pieces
Radish, broccoli, or other small sprouts
Raisins, dried cranberries, or other dried fruit/berry
Crumbled bacon

Kimchee: a wonderful spicy treat

Stretcher

This one is optional. I utilize this only if I am short on the meat component.

>Grain such as cooked rice, barley, quinoa, etc.
>Bean such as pinto, black, lentil, etc.

Feel free to double up (or triple, if needed) on the crunch and/or treat.

Amounts

I want to have about a cup of salad per adult-size serving, and since I am making a meat salad, I want that to be the bulk of it.

Guesstimate a bit more than a ½ cup of meat (or combination with the stretcher) per person.

Figure about ¼ cup of crunch per person, and a couple tablespoons of treat.

The sauce is added until it is, well, saucy enough. The amount of sauce you like may be more or less than we like (we do like our salads on the saucy side).

Seasoning is also done to your taste.

Putting It All Together

Mix up the meat (and stretcher if using), crunch, and treat. Then add sauce and seasoning(s).

Be sure to taste it to make sure it's perfect. If not, you may need more sauce or more/different seasonings.

You may need to add a little honey or Sucanat to the salad and then counteract that sweetness with apple cider vinegar. This gives a slightly sweet and sour flavor.

Tip: If I'm using honey, I premix it with the sauce before adding into the salad. It combines better that way. I find it kind of fun to play with the flavors, and hopefully end up with something slightly new and different.

Serve It

We like our meat salads served on a bed of mixed greens. We sometimes drizzle a homemade salad dressing over the top.

I've also experimented with putting our meat salads on top of a grain base (if I didn't use a stretcher). This works pretty well and makes a very hearty meal. Quinoa, brown rice, spelt, sprouted wheat, and sprouted lentil all make great salad bases.

Tasty Combinations

- Chicken, apple, green onion, mayonnaise, curry, salt, and pepper
- Beef, broccoli, raisins, bacon (turkey), mayonnaise, Sucanat, apple cider vinegar, salt, and pepper
- Tuna, cucumber, green onion, buttermilk dressing, smidgen of mustard, salt, pepper, celery seed
- Beef, celery, avocado, mayonnaise, smidgen of mustard, salt, pepper, basil

Basic Meat Salad Method

½ cup of meat per person
Stretcher (optional; only if needed to add to meat so it equals ½ cup per person)

¼ cup of crunch (plus or minus) per person
2 tablespoons of treat (plus or minus) per person
Sauce, as much or as little as you like
Seasoning, to taste

Mix all ingredients together.

Serve on a bed of greens or grains.

Add a little extra sauce if desired.

Roast Beef and Almond Spread on Veggies

Variation: Meat Spread

This is great served on crackers, vegetable coins, or bread.

Cut meat, crunch, and treat smaller than you would when making the salad version. You may need a little extra sauce.

Be sure to give it a really good mixing to achieve spread consistency.

So quick, so easy, and so good!

Design a Salad Dressing

One of the quickest and easiest ways to improve your diet is to stop buying commercially prepared salad dressing. These dressings are made with awful ingredients that you don't want to put into your body.

What kind of awful ingredients, you ask?

For starters, they're made with low-quality oils—often soy and/or canola—preservatives, high-fructose corn syrup, MSG, and a whole host of possible additives.

Ditching store-bought dressings is especially easy since it only takes a couple of minutes to mix up your own homemade salad dressing with your choice of healthy ingredients.

While I have found some great recipes for salad dressings, I tend to just throw things together with whatever we have on hand.

These still taste great, even though they may not fall into a dressing category that you can name! I tend to think of these as House Dressings. ☺ These are creamy dressings that use a cream-style base. Think ranch dressing, only better and changeable to whatever you have on hand.

Ingredients

Base: I like to mix at least two bases together, but I've had great results with more than two when I only have a smidge of this or that.

These are suggestions based on what I've tried, but you might think of other things.

I like to make my salad dressings in pint-size jars. Then I fill that jar about half full with my base(s) and then build from there. This way, I have plenty of room for mixing and adding.

You could start with a larger or smaller jar/container; just keep in mind the space needed for stirring and adding additions.

Start with any of the following bases:

- Mayonnaise (homemade, lacto-fermented is best)
- Buttermilk
- Kefir
- Yogurt
- Clabber
- Clabber cheese
- Kefir cheese
- Yogurt cheese
- Soft cheese
- Cream cheese
- Sour cream
- Sweet cream (raw)
- Ketchup (lacto-fermented or at least high-fructose corn syrup free)
- Olive oil (see note)
- Barbeque sauce, teriyaki sauce, or another similar item

Note: When using olive oil, for better blending, mix as you add the oil. Use a fork or a small whisk. This will help it all emulsify better.

If adding lemon juice in addition to olive oil (for the Creamy Vinaigrette), I've found it blends best when mixing in the lemon juice prior to the olive oil.

Seasoning, Spices, and Herbs: Think about the final flavor you want. Maybe you want to go for a certain theme. With a taco-style salad, you'd use taco flavorings and/or add salsa (see Additions).

With Asian, you may add garlic and ginger. Greek: garlic and oregano.

At the very least, add sea salt.

Other seasonings to consider are dill, powdered or minced garlic, basil, mint, cumin, chili powder, cayenne pepper, black pepper, parsley (fresh or dried), mustard powder, etc.

Sometimes I'll add a little bit of Sucanat to my dressing. Oftentimes, this is added after I put everything else in it and I've tasted it.

If you taste your dressing and you think, "Hmmm…something is missing," you might add ½ to 1 teaspoon of Sucanat or another sweetener. And maybe another sprinkling of salt. Those are the two things I find help my dressings the most.

Additions: I don't always do an addition, but it's a nice way to change up the flavors. Add anywhere from 1 tablespoon on up. I've had good results going as high as equal amounts addition to base. Especially when using salsa.

Salsa, combined with the base, makes a wonderful dressing for Taco Salad. If I'm using a "runny" salsa, I drain it a bit first. (My lacto-fermented salsa can get a little runny.)

Other excellent additions include minced onion, finely chopped green onions, finely chopped sweet pepper, finely chopped hot pepper, grated cucumber, pickle relish (or probably any vegetable relish), shredded Parmesan cheese or other hard cheese, crumbled blue cheese, poppy seed, honey, or a prepared mustard such as Dijon or other flavor.

Flavorings/Thinners: Sometimes my dressing is a little bit too thick. Especially if I've started with a thicker base such as clabber cheese. When this happens, I add in a thinner.

Sometimes these double as a flavor addition; keep that in mind when choosing your thinner. For zero to very little flavor, use milk, cream, or even water. Other thinners can be lemon juice, vinegar (any flavor), kombucha, or the juice from a lacto-fermented pickle, kraut, or salsa.

Tasty Combinations

>**Creamy Vinaigrette:** Yogurt or buttermilk, lemon juice, olive oil, sea salt, and pepper. Simple and delicious. (See the *Note* in the Base section on using Olive oil.)

Garlic/Dill: Mayonnaise and buttermilk or yogurt, ample amount of powdered garlic, dill weed, sea salt, a dash of Sucanat, and apple cider vinegar.

Something like Thousand Island: Ketchup, mayonnaise (or yogurt), pickle relish, and sea salt.

Basic Salad Dressing Method

Base, enough to fill your container no more than half
Seasoning, to taste
Additions (optional; 1+ tablespoons)
Flavorings/thinners (optional)

Put base in chosen container, then add seasoning, additions and/or flavorings.

Mix well. Taste and adjust as needed.

Variation: Dip

Use the same concept and ingredients as salad dressing, but keep it on the thick side and go easy on or eliminate the thinner entirely. Goes great with crackers or vegetable sticks.

Design a...?

A few years back, my family lived in an itsy-bitsy camp trailer for eight months when our house sold faster than we expected and we didn't yet have a house in Wyoming.

During that time, most of our meals were simple, one-dish skillet meals. These were often constructed (or should I say, concocted) while standing at the stove or electric skillet.

We were at the very beginning of our real food journey at that time, but we still enjoyed some wonderful and wholesome dishes.

I cooked so many of these skillet dishes that it was quite some time before I could bring myself to construct skillet dishes again! I needed a break.

Truthfully, even though we created many of these skillet dishes, I'm not the expert in this area. Wardee from Traditional Cooking School holds this title (I crowned her myself). Be sure to look in the Resources section for a link to this terrific information—you'll definitely want to add it to your formula collection.

What Other Things Work Well With Formulas?

Just about anything! We make cheese dips and spreads, baked oatmeal, beans in a variety of flavors that are easily changed (aka: Stretchy Beans), and even lacto-fermented items—just by following a few simple "rules." Once you get comfortable with this style of cooking, you have a ton of options.

And, yes, once in a while, you may have a dish turn out not quite as you wished. When that happens, just remember what you did and don't repeat it. ☺ Lots of times you'll have a dish turn out excellent. Write that one down.

More on Toppers

I know I've mentioned these a lot. I feel very strongly that the simple addition of a topper to an average dish will elevate it to something special. But my main motivation for toppers is adding lacto-fermented and cultured foods to our meals.

My children just think they're putting some (lacto-fermented) salsa on their dish, but I know they're getting all the great benefits that this probiotic-rich food provides.

Probiotics contain many beneficial organisms that are good for our gut health. But let me tell you, my children love my salsa and eat it like candy—never even stopping to notice just how good it is for them. In fact, my husband recently suggested we hide it so he can get a serving or two before the jar runs empty!

There are many lacto-fermented items available commercially (Bubbies is one brand that I can buy locally) or you can make your own. Once you start making your own and discover just how easy it is, you'll love it. Many cultured products are also available commercially; again, making your own is quite easy and very rewarding.

I highly recommend the Traditional Cooking School by GNOWFGLINS's eCourses or eBooks if you are interested in learning how to make your own cultured dairy and lacto-fermented products. You'll love the way the lessons are taught.

More From Millie Copper

Get 20% off Millie Copper's other nonfiction books at HomespunOasis.com/Books with coupon code SAVE20.

Stretchy Beans: Nutritious, Economical Meals the Easy Ways

Do you struggle with feeding your family delicious, healthy meals? Are you tired of trying to figure out what's for dinner each night? Do you cringe when you see how much money your family spends on groceries each month?

If so, *Stretchy Beans* is the solution you've been looking for! Learn how to easily prepare dinners that the whole family will love—while staying on budget, spending less time in the kitchen, and not losing your sanity.

Real Food Hits the Road: Budget-Friendly Tips, Ideas, and Recipes for Enjoying Real Food Away from Home

Are you planning to hit the road for a family vacation? Do you want to take a road trip, but the idea of eating out three meals a day doesn't work for your budget or your health?

Real Food Hits the Road will be your guide to saving the budget, keeping your digestion working well, and eating real food away from home while letting you enjoy the trip and not "cook" all of the time.

Stock the Real Food Pantry: Save Money and Time While Gaining Peace of Mind

Do you want to stock your pantry with nutritious food your family will actually eat? In these trying times, are you focusing on your food storage?

If so, *Stock the Real Food Pantry* has you covered. Learn how a wonderfully stocked real food pantry will save you money and time—while giving you peace of mind.

Resources

Books

The Complete Tightwad Gazette by Amy Dacyczyn

Nourishing Traditions by Sally Fallon and Mary Enig

Blogs and Websites

Traditional Cooking School by GNOWFGLINS

Cooking Traditional Foods by KerryAnn Foster

Nourished Kitchen by Jenny McGruther

Weston A. Price Foundation

Money-Saving Tips, Tricks, and Ideas

Use Your Freezer! Stash leftover rice, vegetables, meats, etc. in the freezer until you have enough to create a dish. Consider having a container that all your leftover vegetables go in, a second one for meats, and a third for grains. (You could mix your grains or add additional containers if you want to keep them separate.)

Just remember that you have these things in your freezer! I know my freezer can be a black hole at times.

Save Bones! We save all of our bones for broth making. Roasted a chicken? Great! Debone it and either immediately turn it into broth or stick the carcass in the freezer until ready to use. Had lamb chops? Great, keep the bones and stash in the freezer to turn into lamb broth.

Yes, that might exceed the ewww factor for some people, but let's face it, good-quality meat is expensive. Saving your bones from this good-quality meat allows you to get double use out of the dollars you spent on it.

Remember, broth is a protein sparer, which allows you to consume expensive meats less often. I make my broth in the crock pot. After getting one batch out, I start a second batch with the same bones. Most of the time, I'll even make a third batch using those same bones. The broth still has excellent nutrition in it, it just doesn't end up as gelatinous.

Save Veggies! Don't buy vegetables to add to your homemade broth. Instead, keep the ends of onions, parsley stems, and celery bits in a container in your freezer. Add these to your broth. I don't use carrots because I think they're too sweet, but many people like them.

Eat Beans! One way we afford high-quality grass-fed meats, traditional fats, real milk, and all the other good foods we eat is by enjoying beans quite often. Sometimes three or four times in one week. We use a concept called Stretchy Beans to create several different meals from one pot of beans.

Don't Sweat It! I do the best I can do to prepare nutritious, nutrient-dense, real/whole/traditional foods for my family on the budget we have. Some days the outcome is stellar! Some days it is less than stellar. Tomorrow is a new day in which to make and prepare the foods that meet my criteria. I try not to sweat the days that are less than stellar and know that, overall, I'm doing the best I can. I leave the rest in God's hands.

Meet the Author

Millie Copper is a Wyoming wife and mama. After reading *Nourishing Traditions* in early 2009, her family began transforming their diet to whole, unprocessed, nutrient-dense foods—a little at a time, while stretching their food dollars.

Millie is passionate about sharing how, with a little creativity, anyone can transition to a real foods diet without overwhelming their food budget.

Millie began blogging at Real Food for Less Money (now HomespunOasis.com) in late 2009 and has amassed a collection of frugal recipes and methods. One of her specialties is cooking with wild game (especially antelope ☺) and creating "Stretchy Beans." In May of 2010, she started a Weston A. Price Chapter to share traditional food, health, and farming with Central Wyoming.

Visit HomespunOasis.com for more information, tips, and tricks on budget-friendly real food recipes, homemaking, homesteading, preparedness, and more.

www.ingramcontent.com/pod-product-compliance
Lightning Source LLC
Chambersburg PA
CBHW020542080526
44583CB00013B/949